Preschool Math Workbook for Toddlers

For Kids Ages 2-4

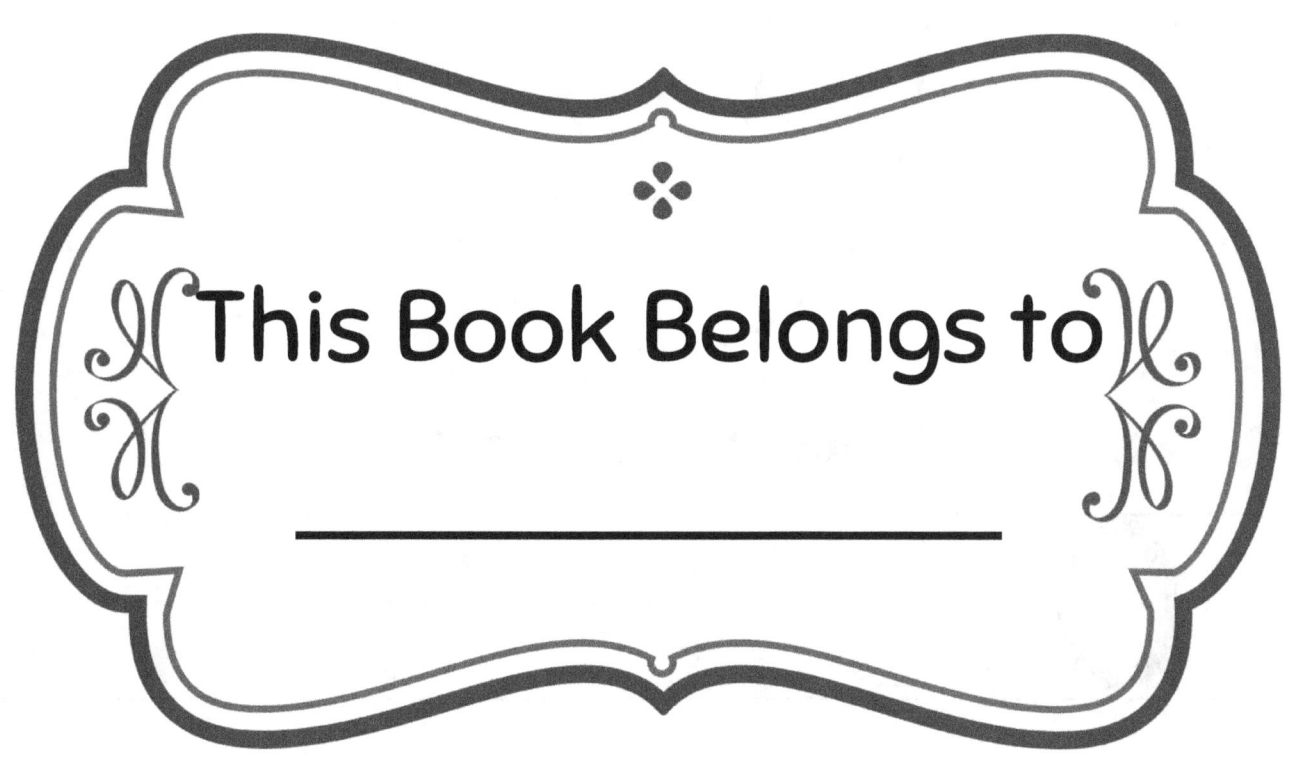

This Book Belongs to

_____

Copyright © 2024

All rights reserved. No part of this publication may be reproduced, distributed, or transmitted in any form or by any means, including photocopying, recording, or other electronic or mechanical methods, without the prior written permission of the publisher.

Tracing Numbers

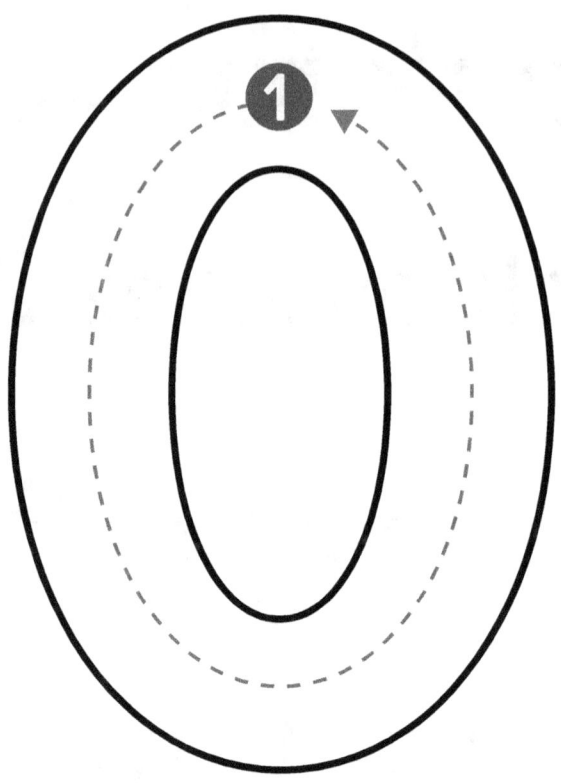

Trace the number 0.

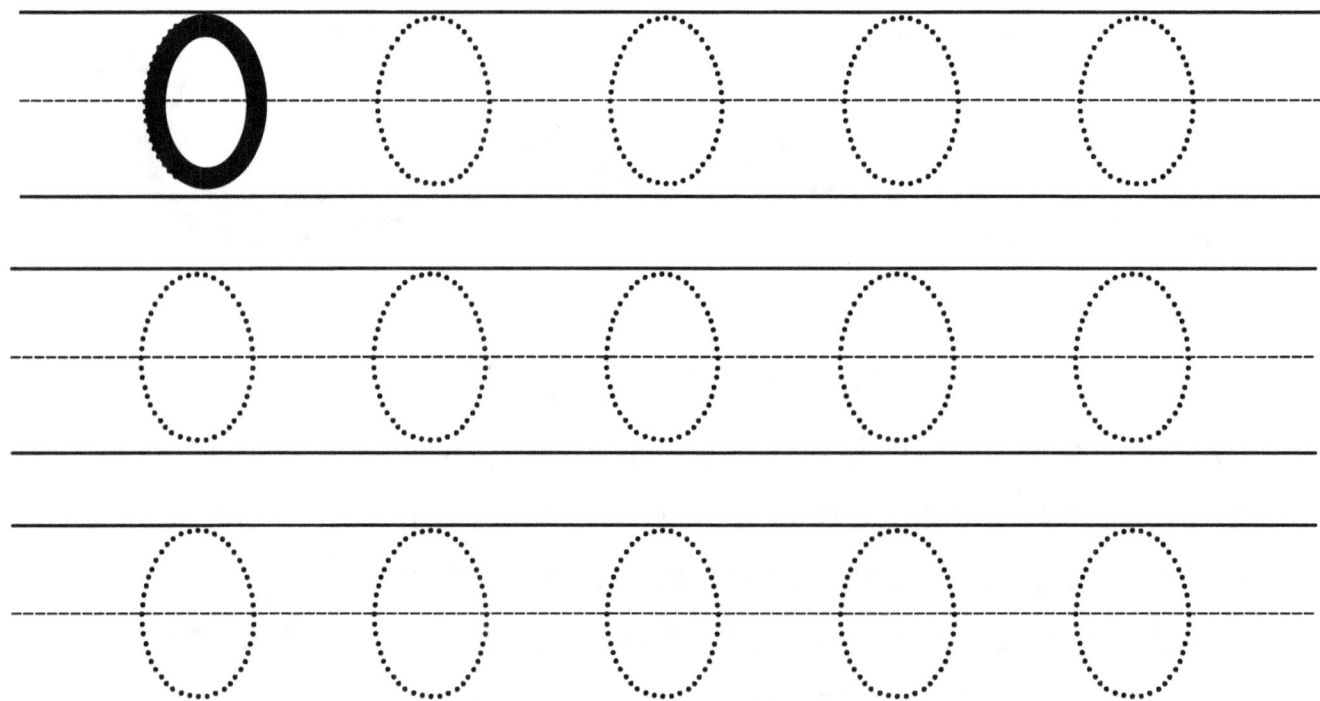

Trace the word zero.

zero zero

zero zero

zero zero

Tracing Numbers

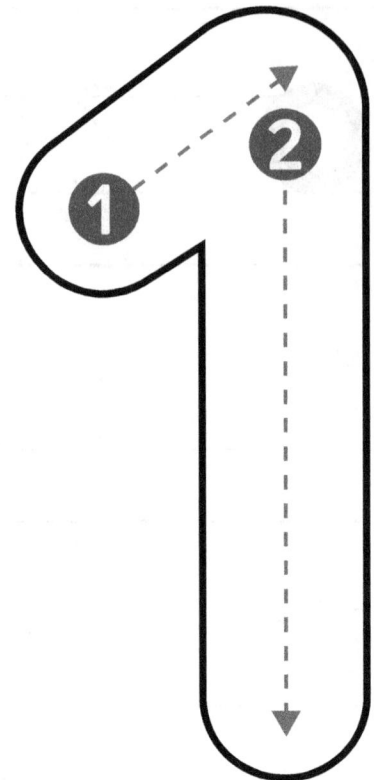

Trace the number 1.

Trace the word one.

one one one

one one one

one one one

Tracing Numbers

Trace the number 2.

2 2 2 2 2

2 2 2 2 2

2 2 2 2 2

Trace the word two.

two two two

two two two

two two two

Tracing Numbers

Trace the number 3.

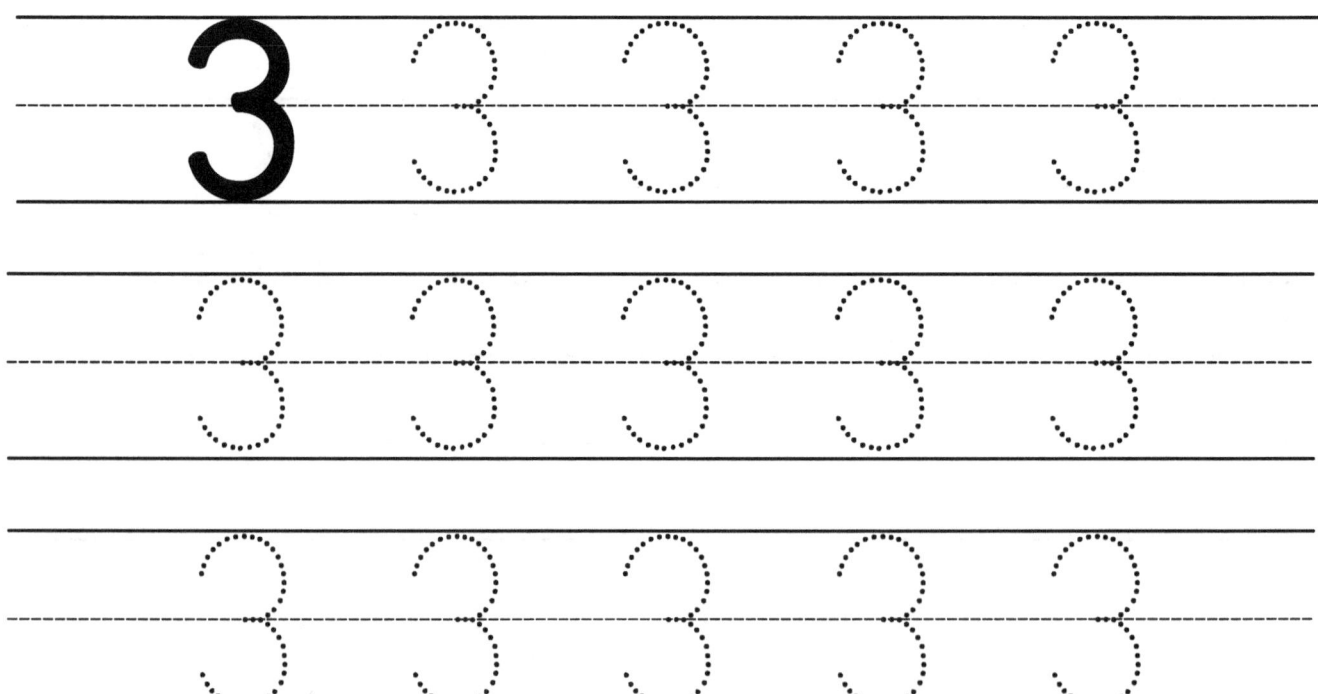

Trace the word three.

three three

three three

three three

Tracing Numbers

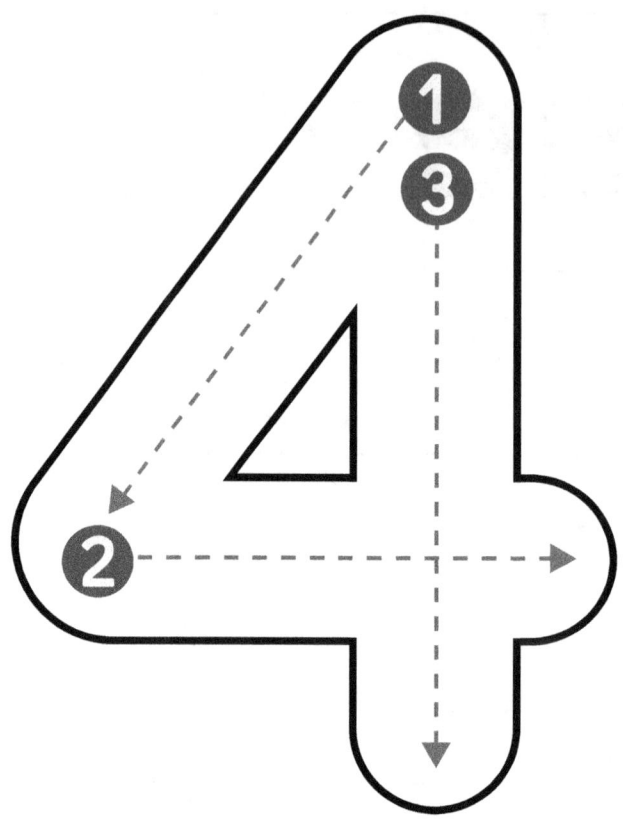

Trace the number 4.

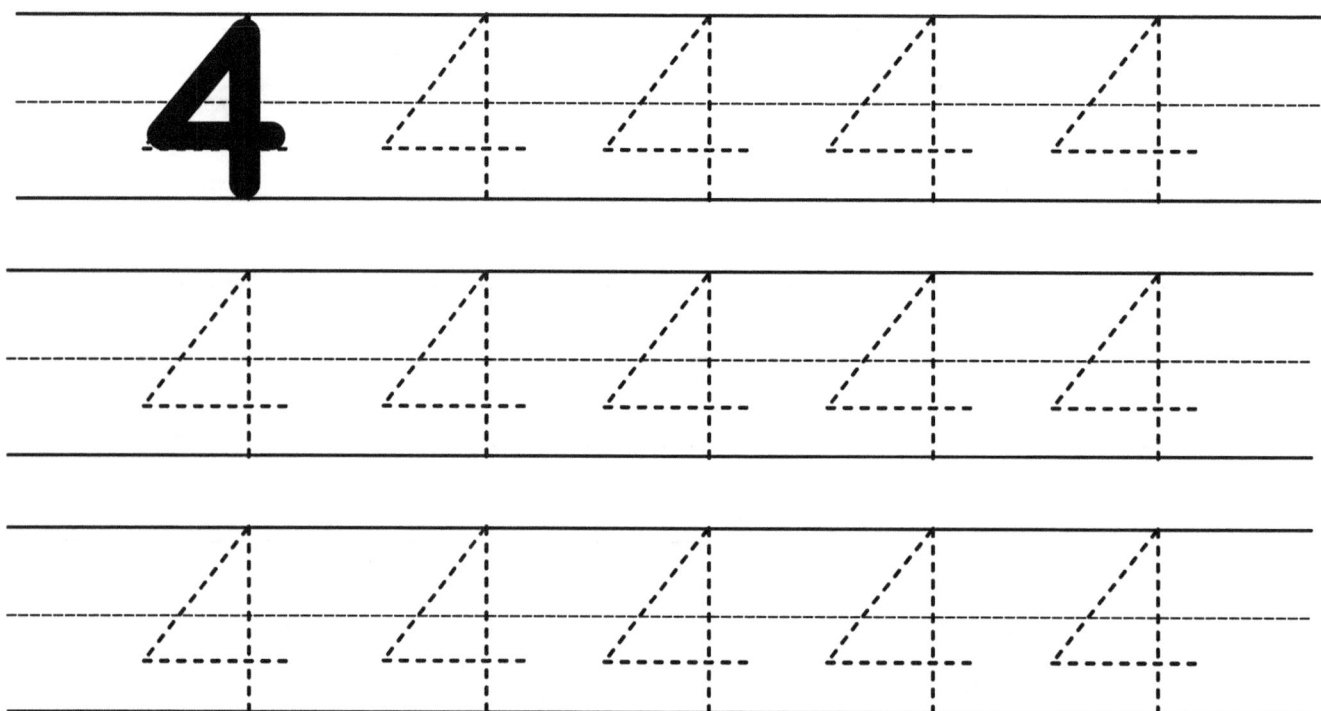

Trace the word four.

Tracing Numbers

Trace the number 5.

Trace the word five.

Tracing Numbers

Trace the number 6.

6 6 6 6 6 6

6 6 6 6 6

6 6 6 6 6

Trace the word six.

six six six

six six six

six six six

Tracing Numbers

Trace the number 7.

Trace the word seven.

seven seven

seven seven

seven seven

Tracing Numbers

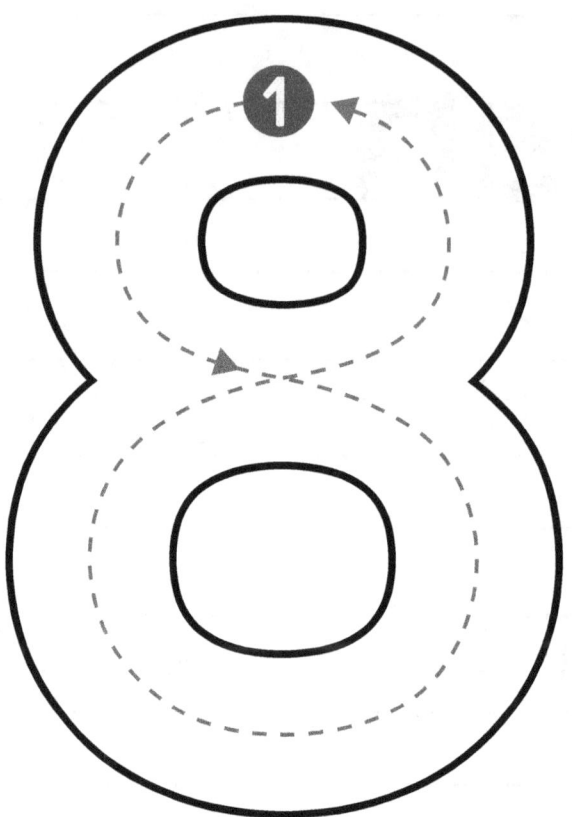

Trace the number 8.

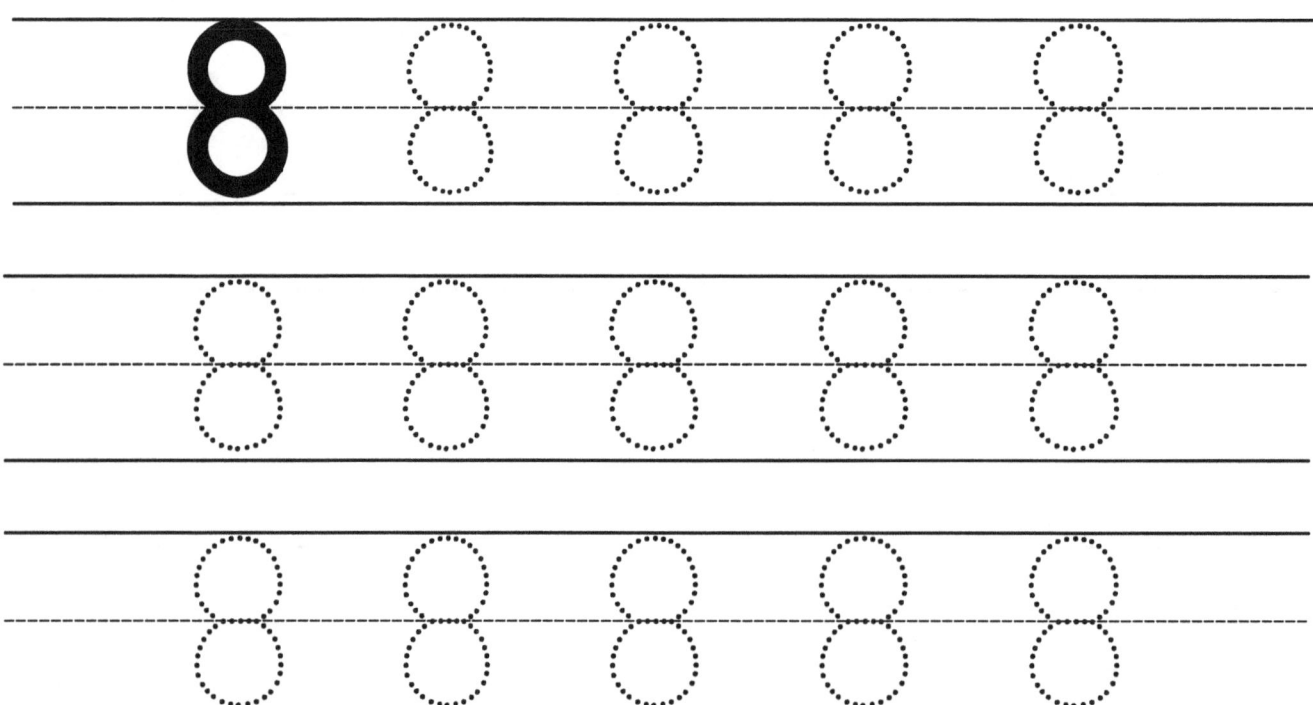

Trace the word eight.

Tracing Numbers

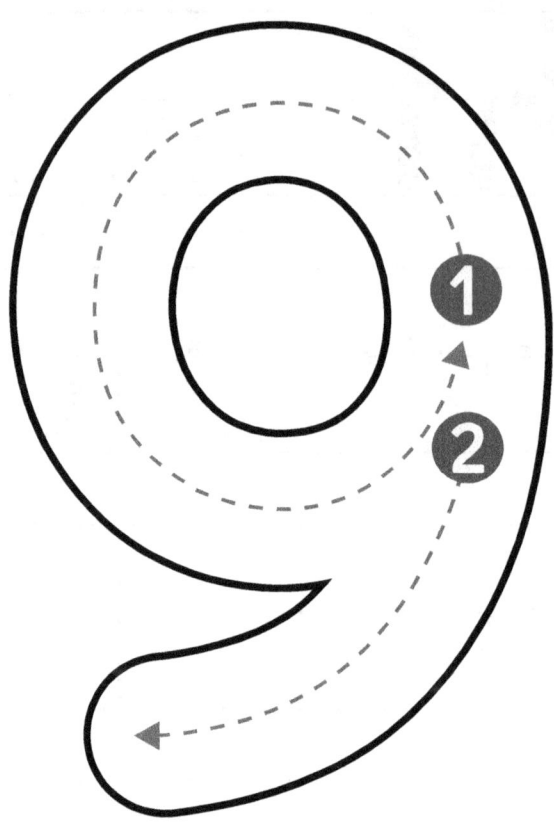

Trace the number 9.

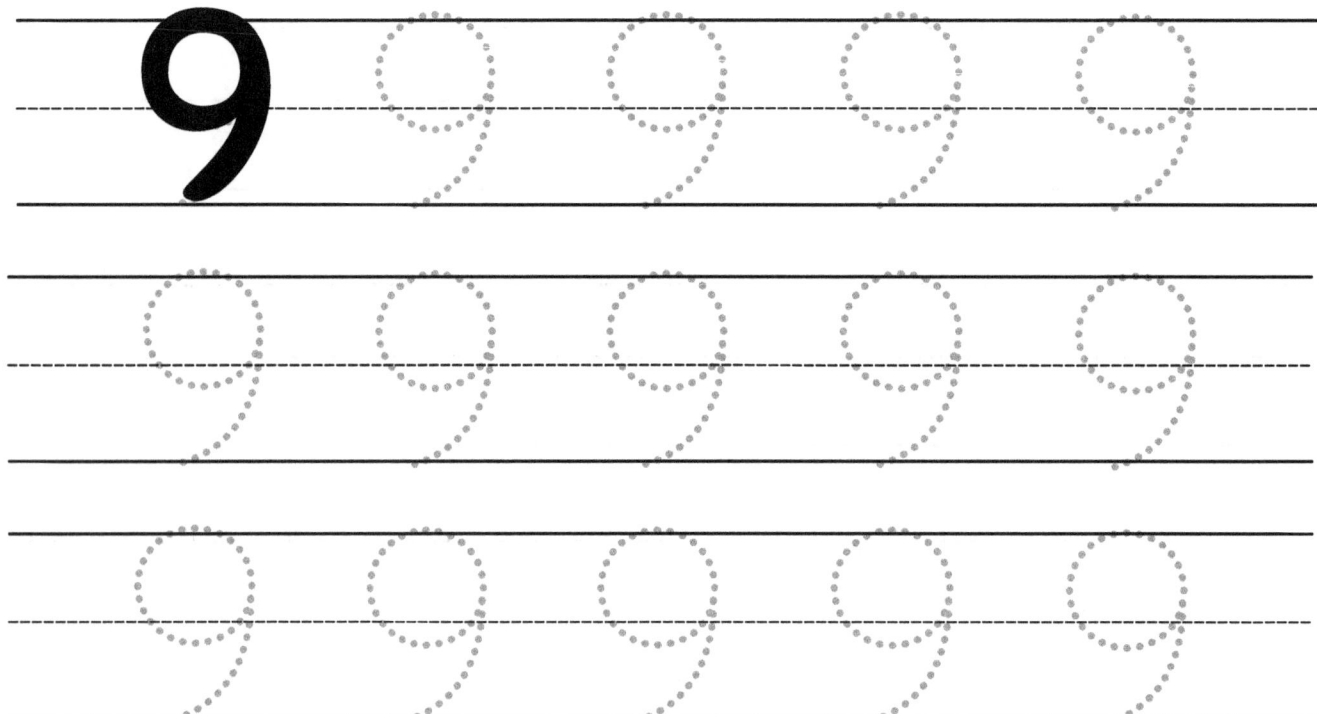

Trace the word nine.

nine nine nine

nine nine nine

nine nine nine

Tracing Numbers

Trace the number 10.

Trace the word ten.

ten ten ten

ten ten ten

ten ten ten

Addition

1 + 2 = _____

4 + 3 = _____

5 + 5 = _____

Addition

5 + 4 = _____

2 + 6 = _____

3 + 7 = _____

Addition

2 + 3 = _____

4 + 6 = _____

3 + 5 = _____

Addition

1 + 4 = ___

3 + 7 = ___

5 + 1 = ___

Addition

8 + 2 = _____

4 + 5 = _____

3 + 5 = _____

Addition

7 + 1 = _____

6 + 4 = _____

10 + 0 = _____

Subtraction

3 - 2 = _____

6 - 4 = _____

10 - 5 = _____

Subtraction

8 - 3 = _____

6 - 6 = _____

7 - 5 = _____

Subtraction

10 − 2 = _____

4 − 3 = _____

9 − 6 = _____

Subtraction

9 - 2 = _____

5 - 4 = _____

7 - 6 = _____

Subtraction

6 − 1 = _____

10 − 4 = _____

8 − 5 = _____

Subtraction

5 - 2 = _____

8 - 4 = _____

7 - 5 = _____

After

Fill in the number after 2.

1   2   ____

Fill in the number after 6.

5   6   ____

Fill in the number after 3.

2   3   ____

Fill in the number after 8.

7   8   ____

After

Fill in the number after 4.

3   4   _____

Fill in the number after 8.

7   8   _____

Fill in the number after 2.

1   2   _____

Fill in the number after 6.

5   6   _____

After

Fill in the number after 6.

5   6   _____

Fill in the number after 5.

4   5   _____

Fill in the number after 4.

3   4   _____

Fill in the number after 7.

6   7   _____

After

Fill in the number after 8.

7   8   _____

Fill in the number after 2.

1   2   _____

Fill in the number after 5.

4   5   _____

Fill in the number after 8.

7   8   _____

After

Fill in the number after 3.

2   3   _____

Fill in the number after 4.

3   4   _____

Fill in the number after 9.

8   9   _____

Fill in the number after 6.

5   6   _____

Before

Fill in the number before 2.

_____   2   3

Fill in the number before 6.

_____   6   7

Fill in the number before 3.

_____   3   4

Fill in the number before 8.

_____   8   9

Before

Fill in the number before 3.

_____ 3 4

Fill in the number before 8.

_____ 8 9

Fill in the number before 4.

_____ 4 5

Fill in the number before 6.

_____ 6 7

Before

Fill in the number before 6.

_____ 6 7

Fill in the number before 5.

_____ 5 6

Fill in the number before 2.

_____ 2 3

Fill in the number before 7.

_____ 7 8

Before

Fill in the number before 4.

_____ 3   4

Fill in the number before 10.

_____ 9   10

Fill in the number before 7.

_____ 6   7

Fill in the number before 6.

_____ 5   6

Before

Fill in the number before 2.

_____ 2 3

Fill in the number before 4.

_____ 4 5

Fill in the number before 7.

_____ 7 8

Fill in the number before 9.

_____ 9 10

Between

Fill in the number between 1 and 3.

1 _____ 3

Fill in the number between 5 and 7.

5 _____ 7

Fill in the number between 2 and 4.

2 _____ 4

Fill in the number between 7 and 9.

7 _____ 9

Between

Fill in the number between 6 and 8.

6 _____ 8

Fill in the number between 7 and 9.

7 _____ 9

Fill in the number between 2 and 5.

2 _____ 5

Fill in the number between 1 and 3.

1 _____ 3

Between

Fill in the number between 5 and 7.

5 _____ 7

Fill in the number between 3 and 5.

3 _____ 5

Fill in the number between 6 and 8.

6 _____ 8

Fill in the number between 2 and 4.

2 _____ 4

Between

Fill in the number between 3 and 5.

3 _____ 5

Fill in the number between 8 and 10.

8 _____ 10

Fill in the number between 1 and 3.

1 _____ 3

Fill in the number between 5 and 7.

5 _____ 7

Between

Fill in the number between 4 and 6.

4 _____ 6

Fill in the number between 2 and 4.

2 _____ 4

Fill in the number between 5 and 7.

5 _____ 7

Fill in the number between 8 and 10.

8 _____ 10

Top and Bottom

Color the picture at the top.

Color the picture at the top.

Color the picture at the bottom.

Color the picture at the bottom.

Top and Bottom

Color the picture at the bottom.

Color the picture at the bottom.

Color the picture at the top.

Color the picture at the top.

—Top and Bottom—

Color the picture at the top.

Color the picture at the bottom.

Color the picture at the bottom.

Color the picture at the top.

Top and Bottom

Color the picture at the bottom.

Color the picture at the top.

Color the picture at the top.

Color the picture at the bottom.

Left and Right

Color the picture on the left.

Color the picture on the right.

Color the picture on the left.

Color the picture on the right.

Left and Right

Color the picture on the right.

Color the picture on the left.

Color the picture on the right.

Color the picture on the left.

Left and Right

Color the picture on the left.

Color the picture on the right.

Color the picture on the right.

Color the picture on the left.

Left and Right

Color the picture on the right.

Color the picture on the left.

Color the picture on the left.

Color the picture on the right..

Big and Small

Color the biggest object.

— Big and Small —

Color the biggest object.

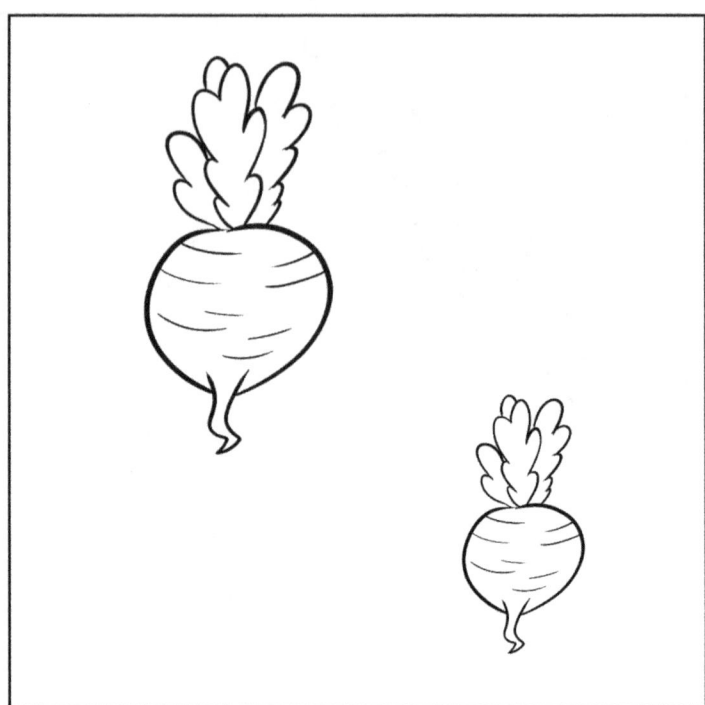

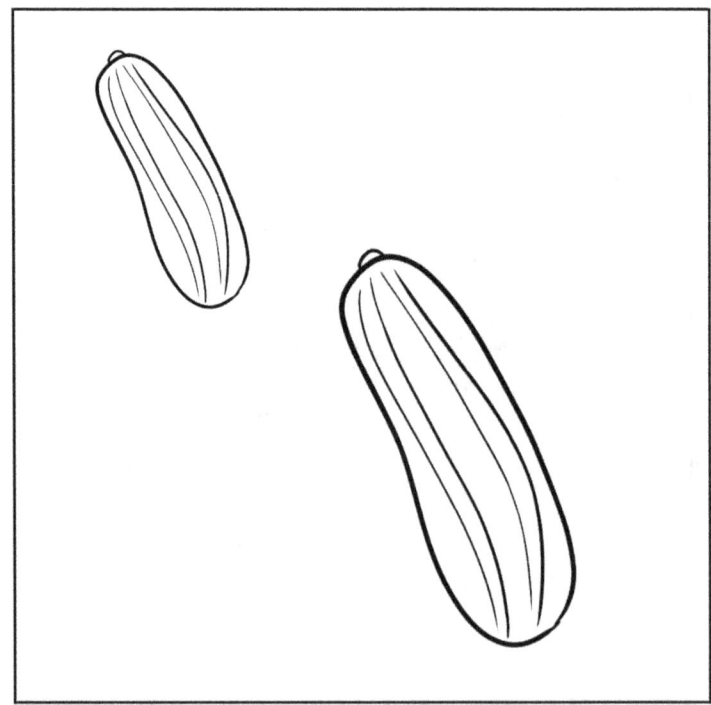

_____

─Big and Small─

Color the smallest object.

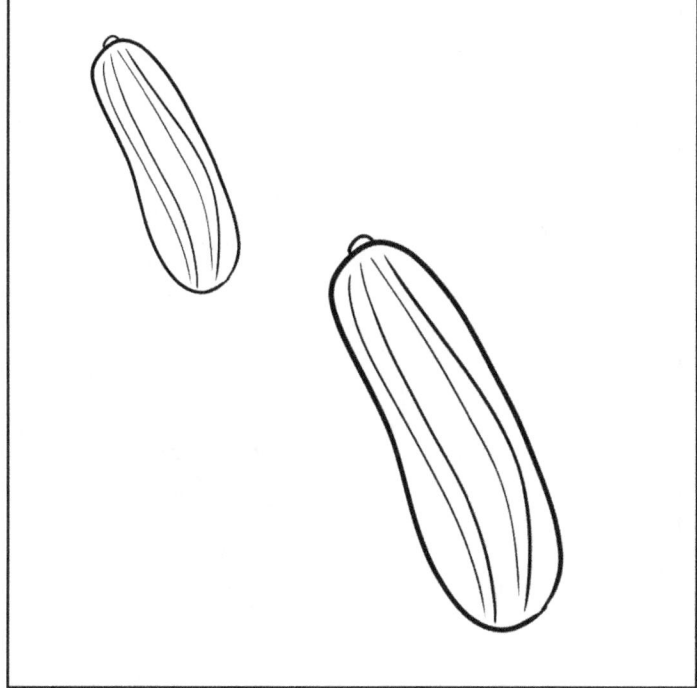

Big and Small

Color the smallest object.

Big and Small

Color the biggest object.

Big and Small

Color the biggest object.

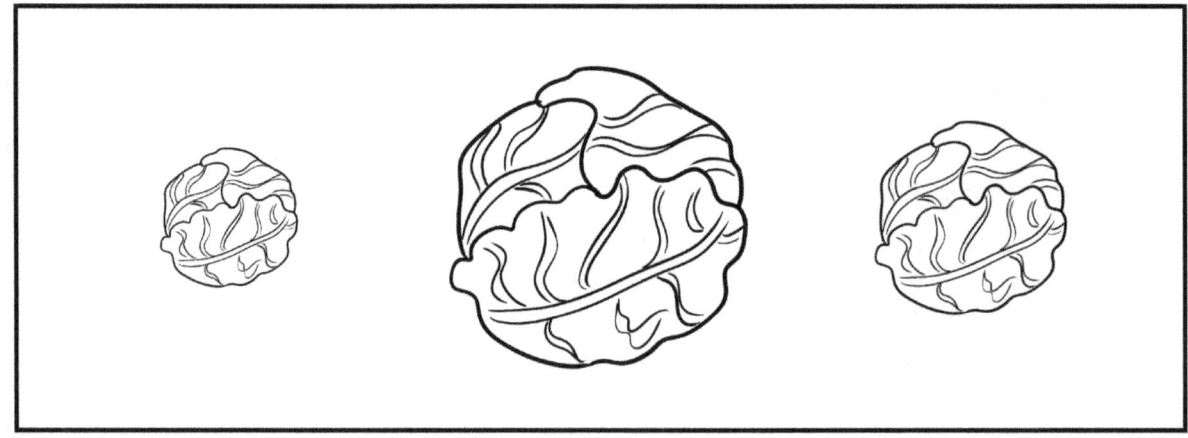

Big and Small

Color the smallest object.

Big and Small

Big and Small

Color the smallest object.

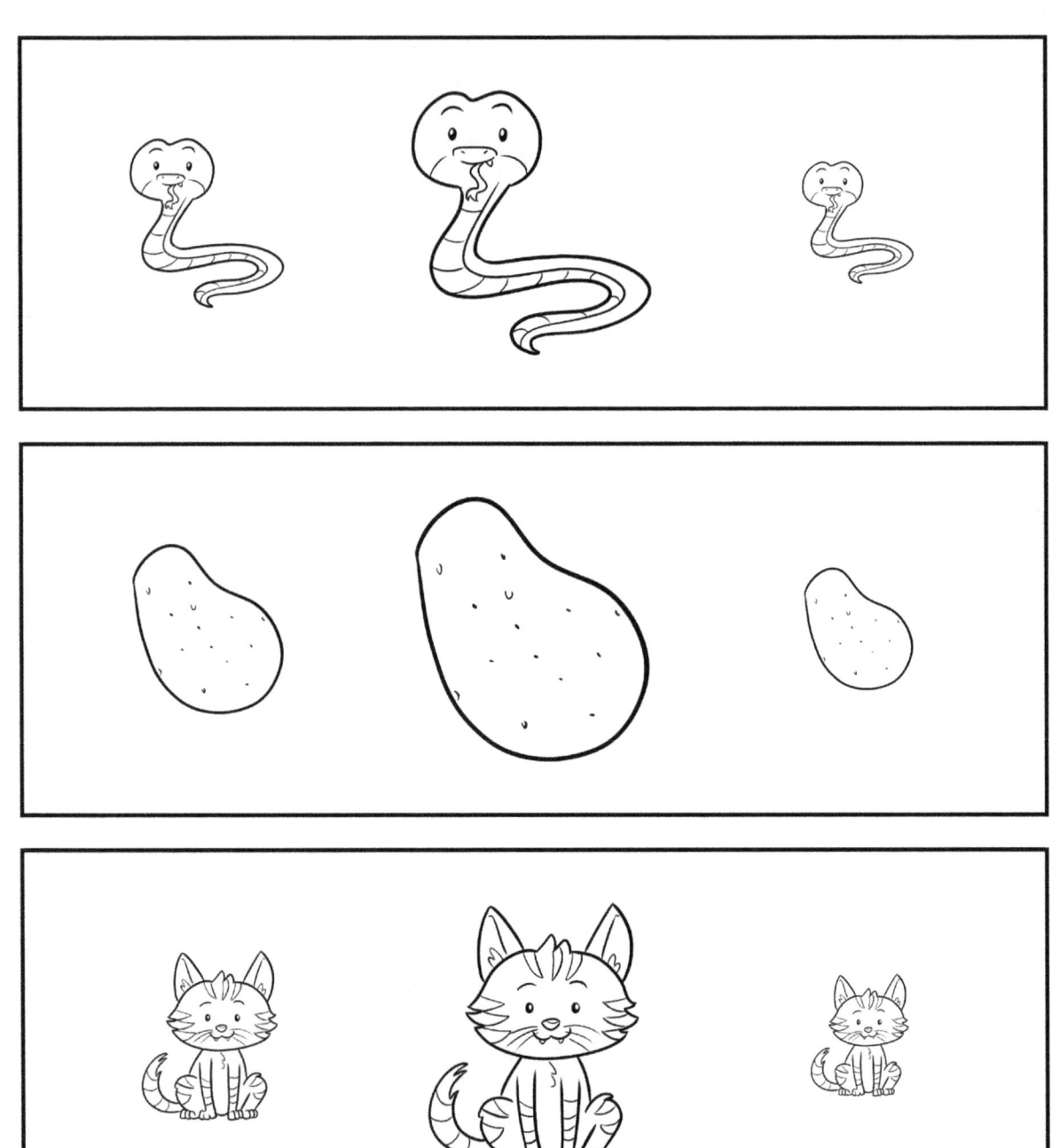

Big and Small

Heavy and Light

Color the heavier object.

Heavy and Light

Color the heavier object.

Heavy and Light

Color the lighter object.

Heavy and Light

Color the lighter object.

How Many

Draw a line to match the pictures to the number.

How Many

Draw a line to match the pictures to the number.

How Many

Draw a line to match the pictures to the number.

How Many

Draw a line to match the pictures to the number.

How Many

Draw a line to match the pictures to the number.

–Color The Number–

Color all the tokens which contain 1.

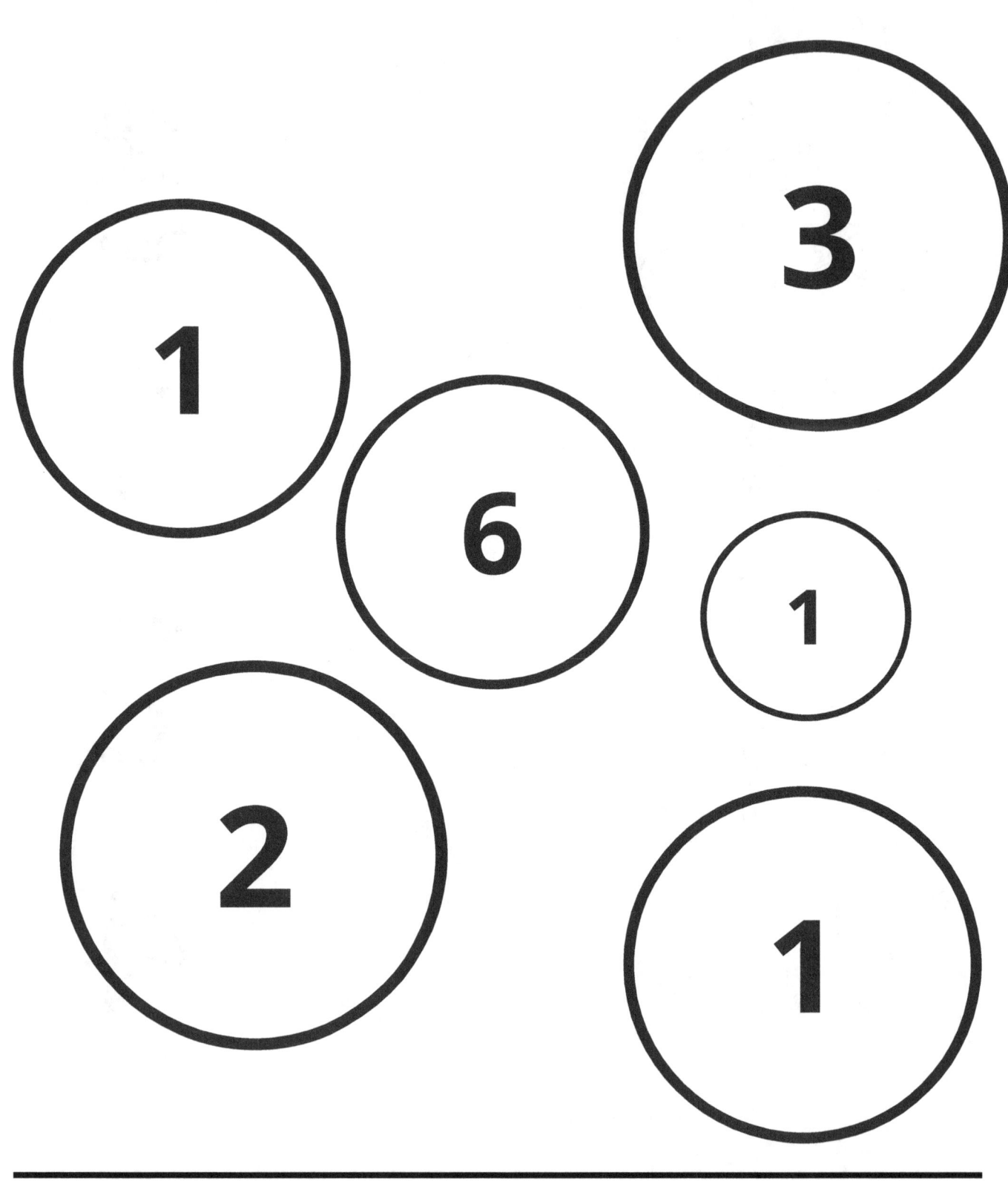

–Color The Number–

Color all the tokens which contain 2.

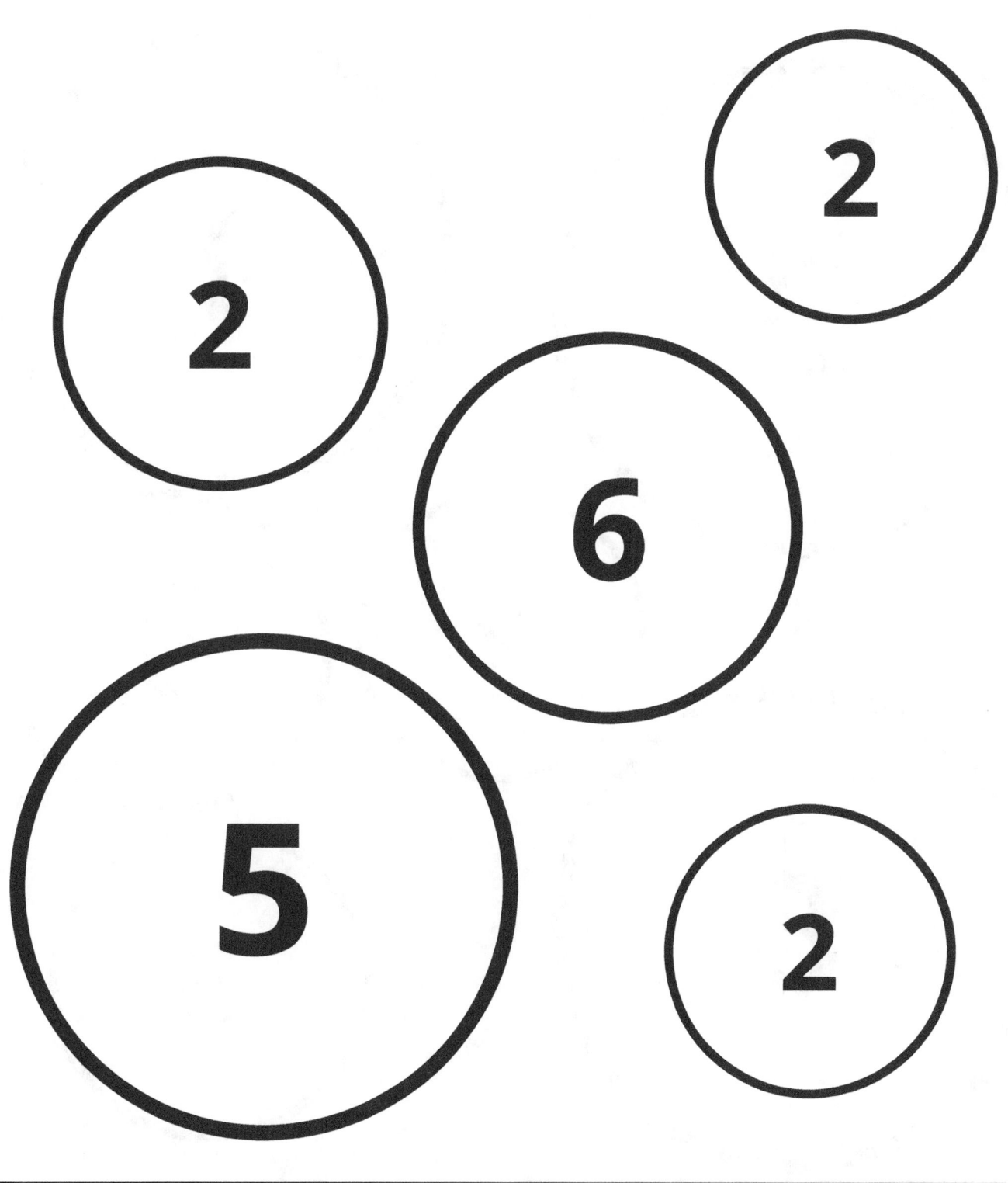

–Color The Number–

Color all the tokens which contain 3.

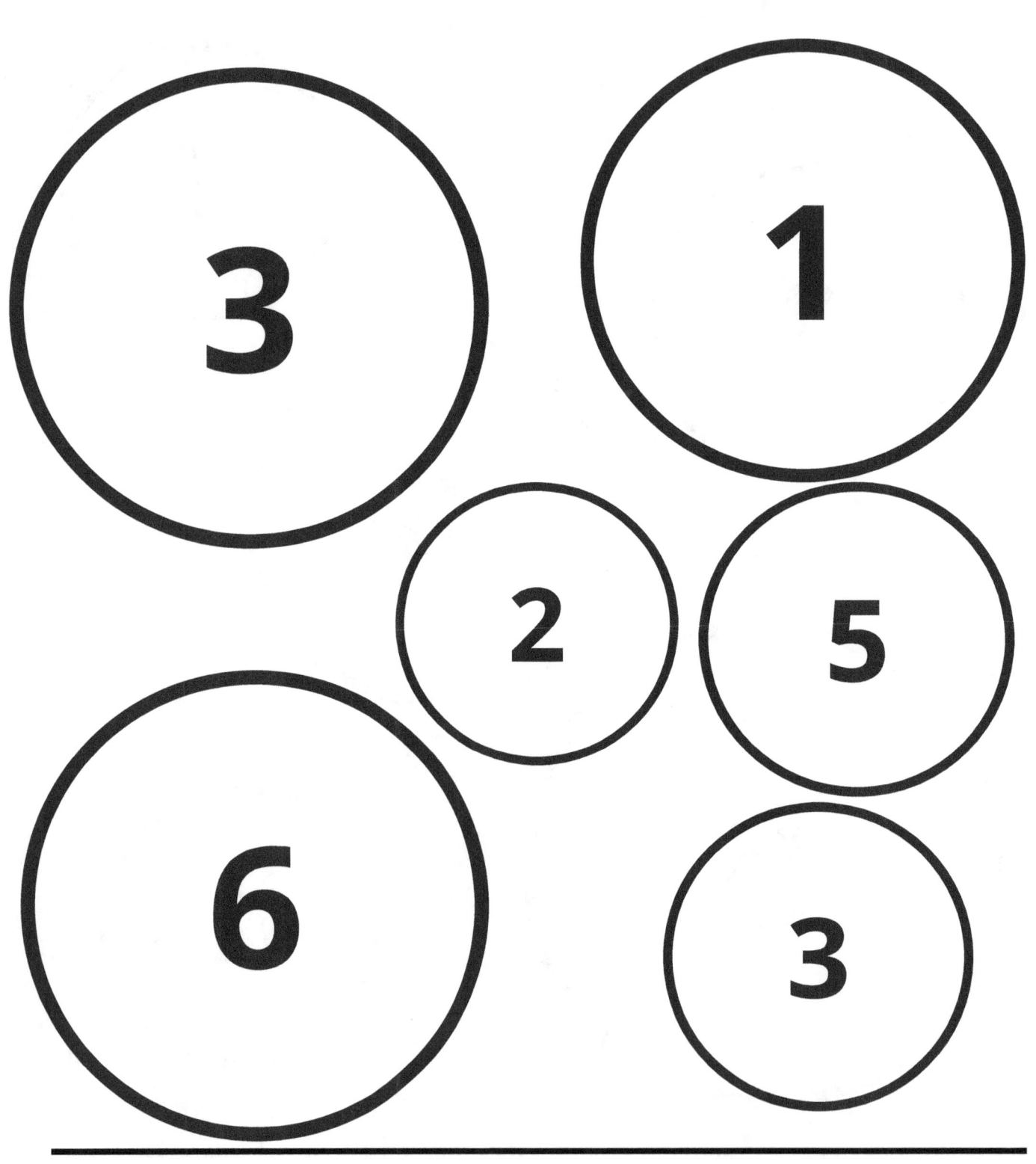

Color The Number

Color all the tokens which contain 4.

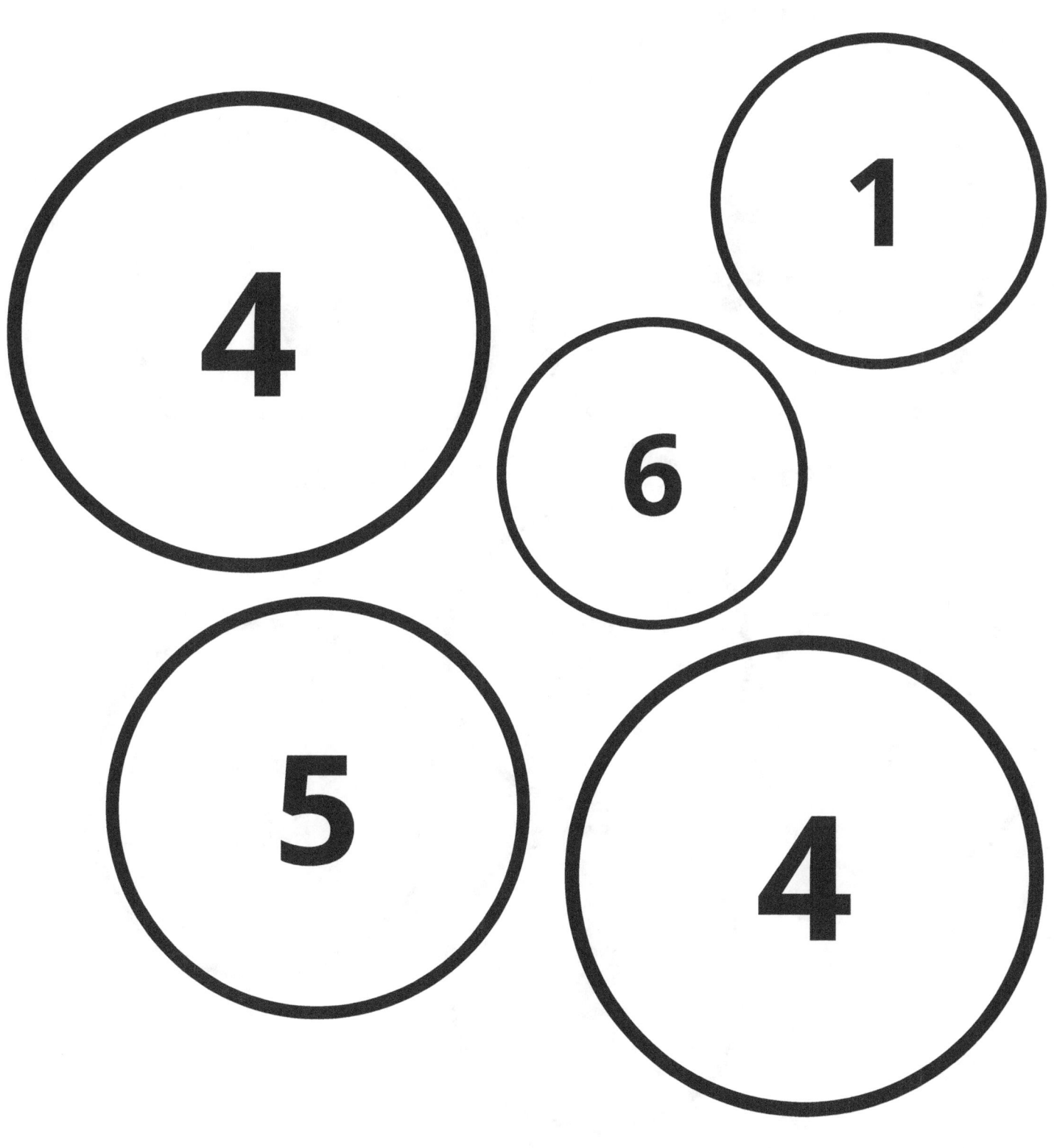

–Color The Number–

Color all the tokens which contain 5.

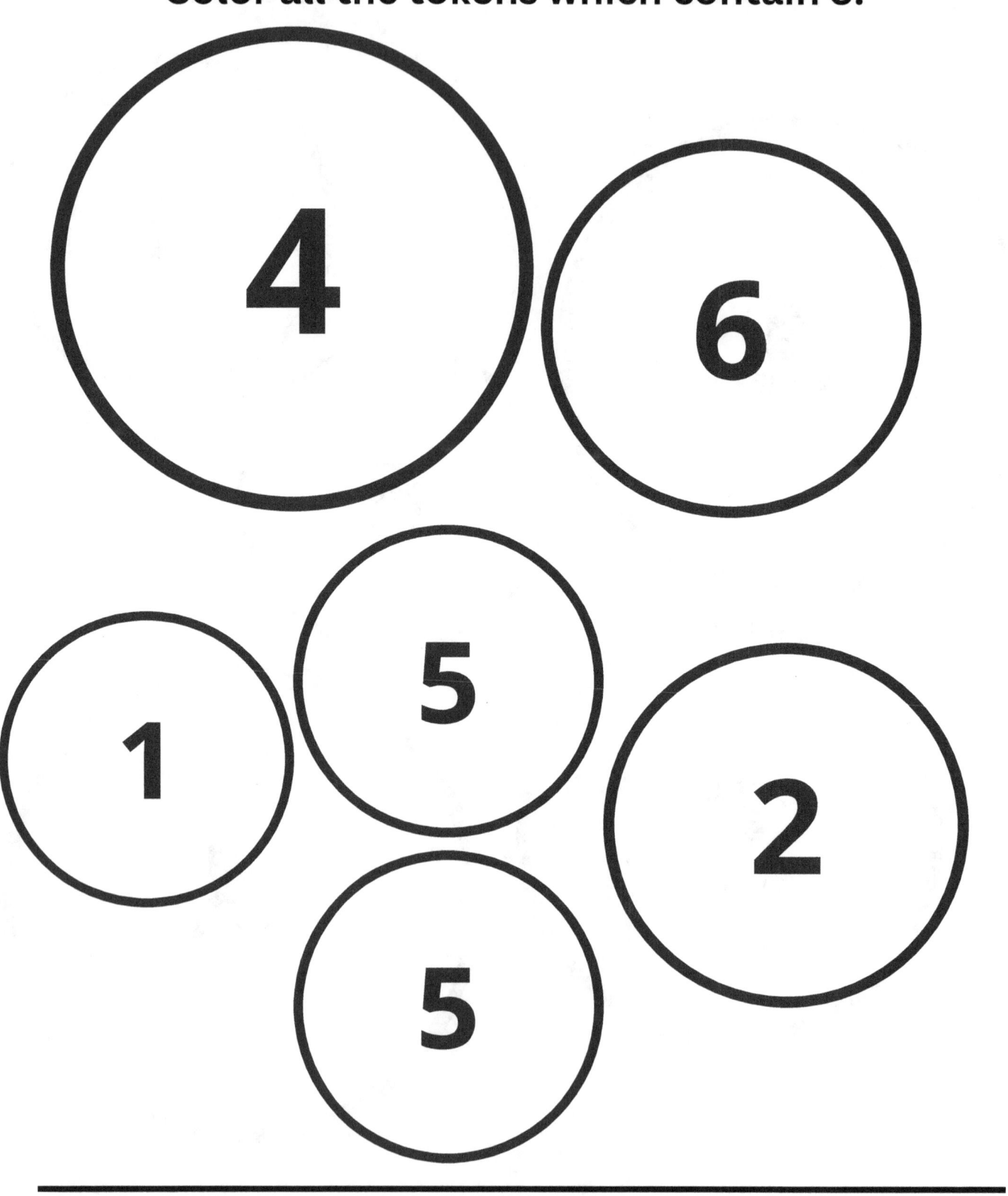

Counting

Count the objects and write the number.

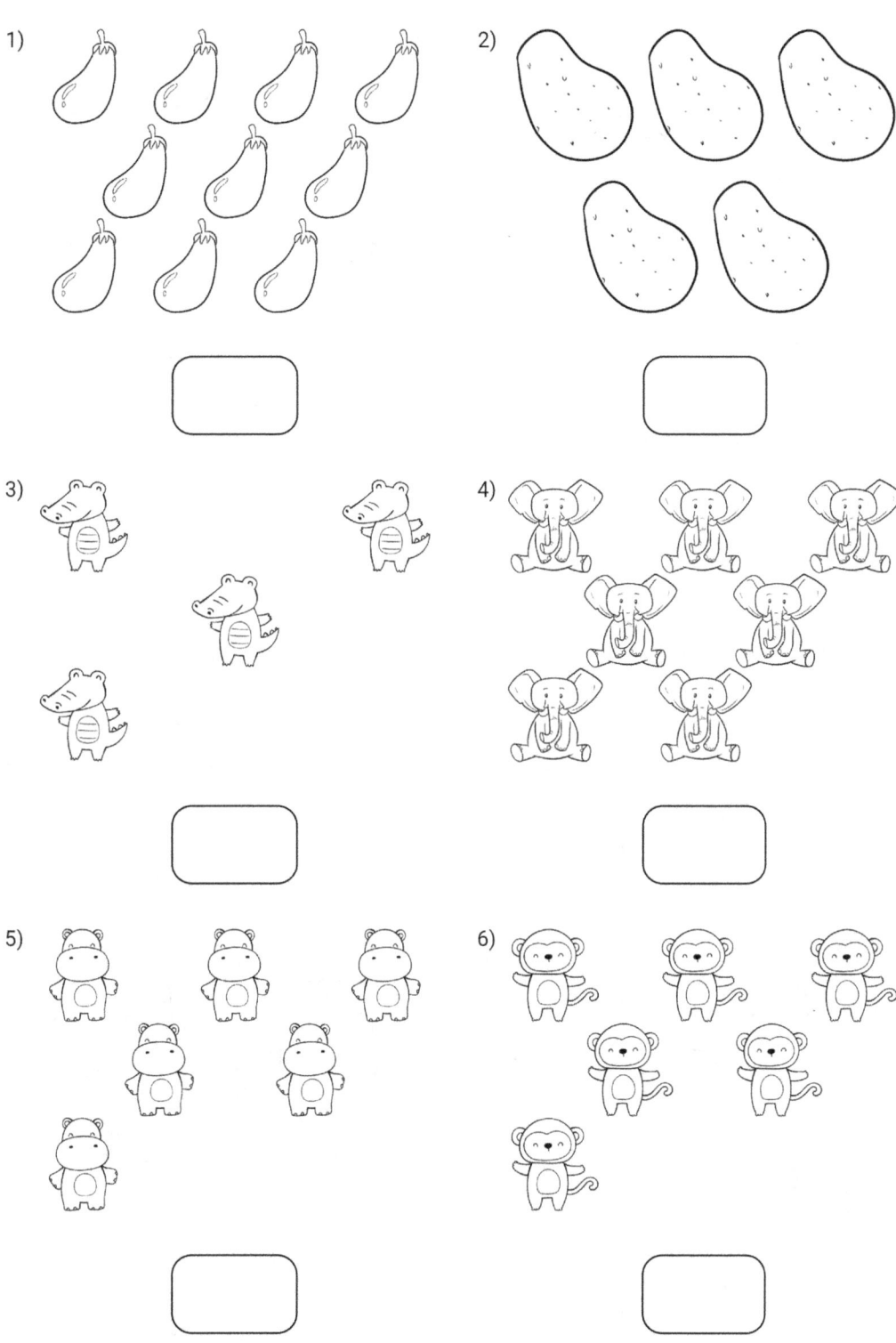

Counting

Count the objects and write the number.

Counting

Count the objects and write the number.

Counting

Count the different types of objects and write the number.

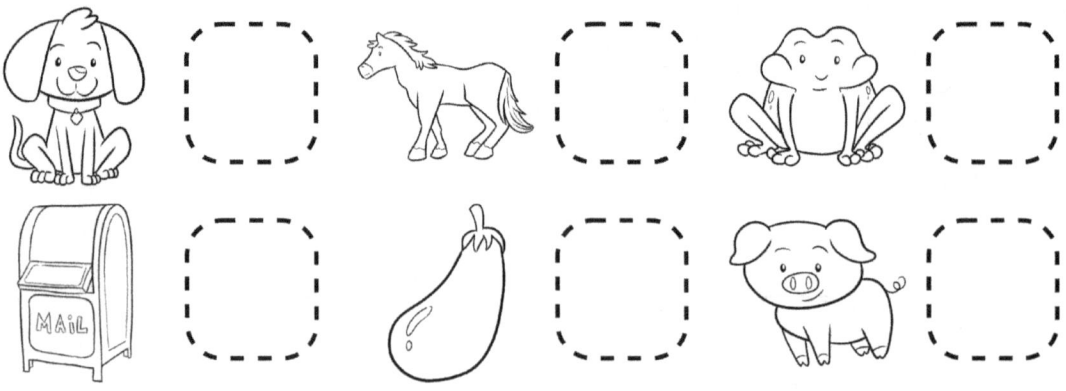

Counting

Count the different types of objects and write the number.

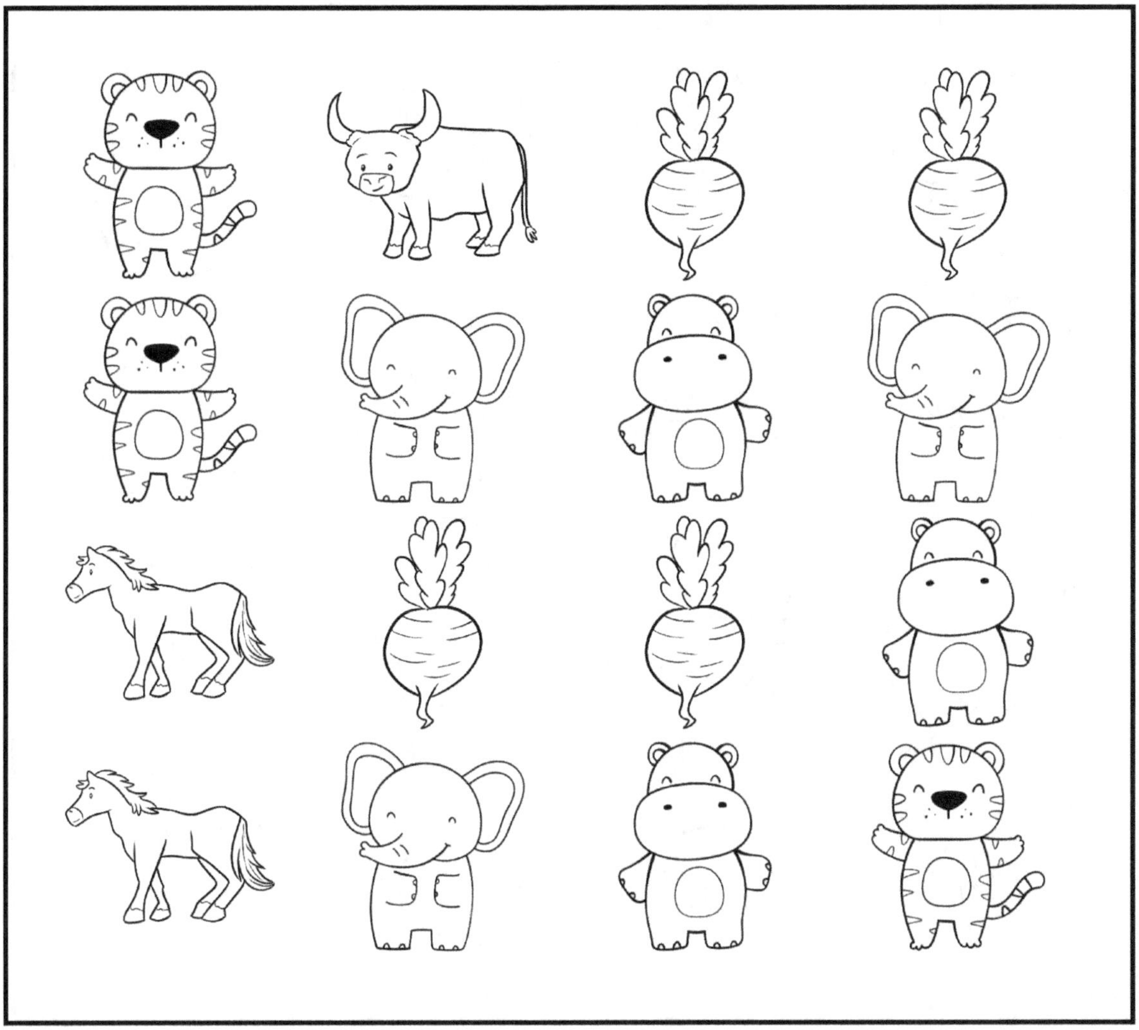

Counting

Count the different types of objects and write the number.

Counting

Count the objects and choose the correct number.

1)

2)

3)

4)

Counting

Count the objects and choose the correct number.

1)

2)
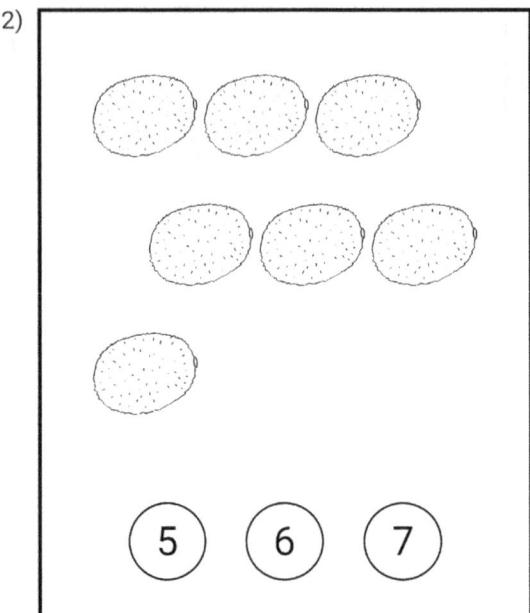

3)

4)
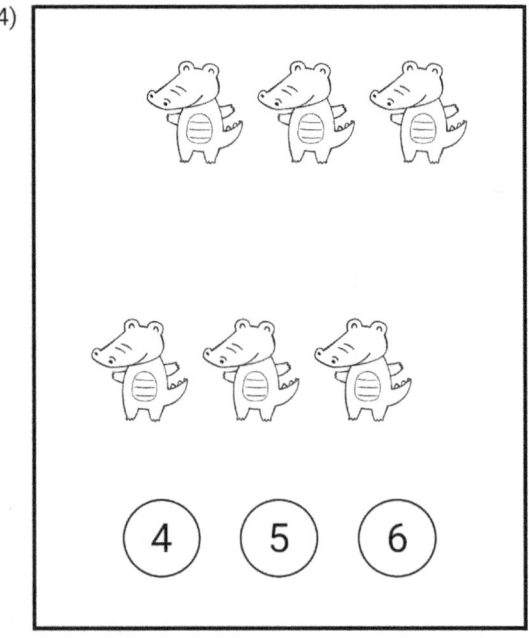

Counting

Count the objects and choose the correct number.

1)

2)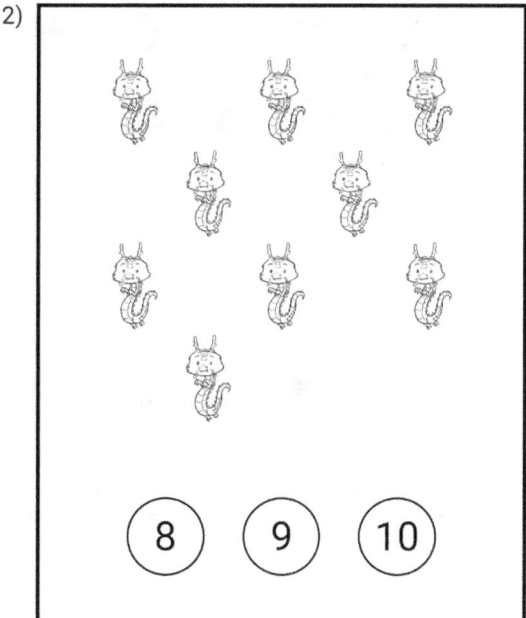

3)

4)

Counting

Count the counters and write the number.

1)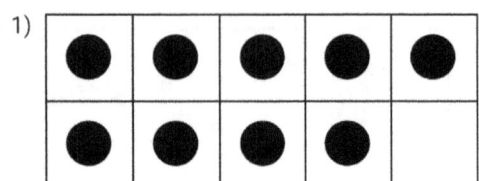

2)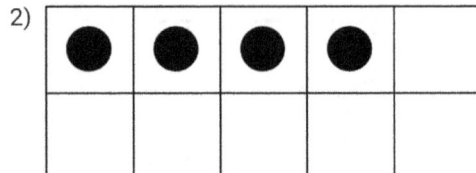

_____ _____

3)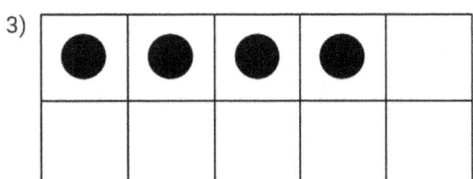

4)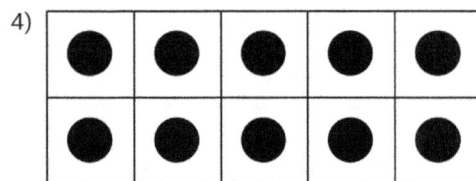

_____ _____

5)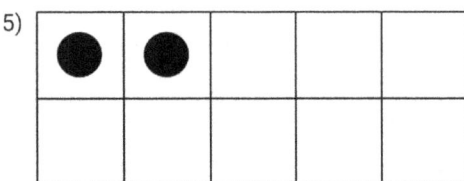

6)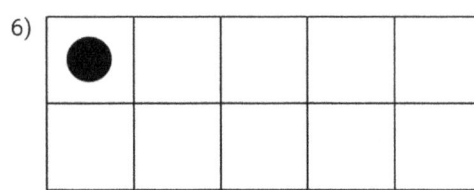

_____ _____

7)

8)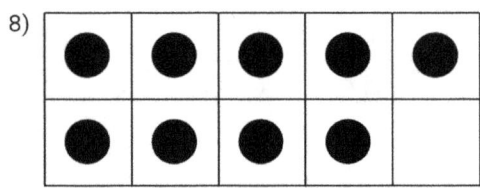

_____ _____

Counting

Count the counters and write the number.

1)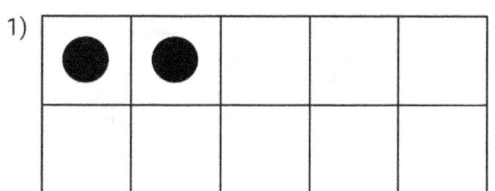

___

2)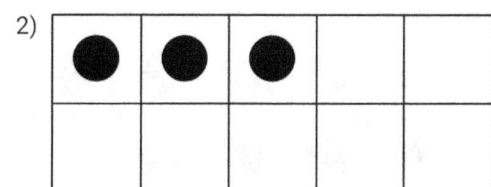

___

3)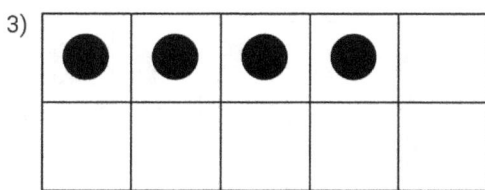

___

4)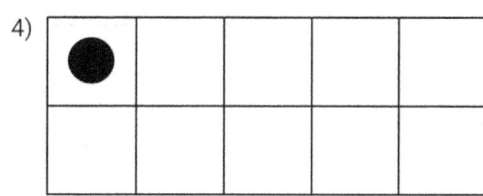

___

5)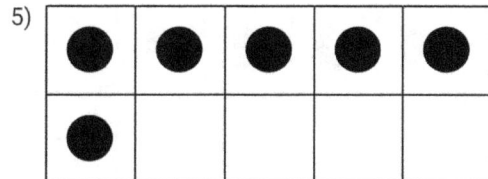

___

6)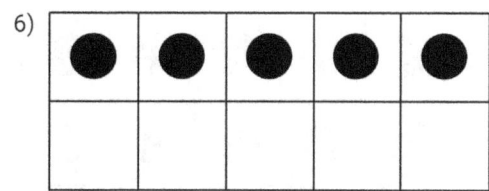

___

7)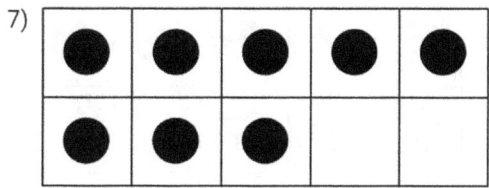

___

8)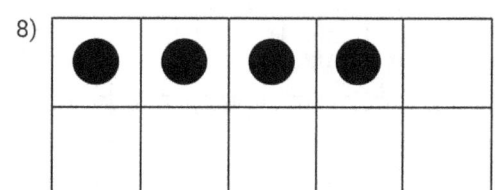

___

Counting

Count the counters and write the number.

1) 9 ___

2) 3 ___

3) 1 ___

4) 7 ___

5) 10 ___

6) 4 ___

7) 2 ___

8) 8 ___

Counting

Color the counters to match the number shown.

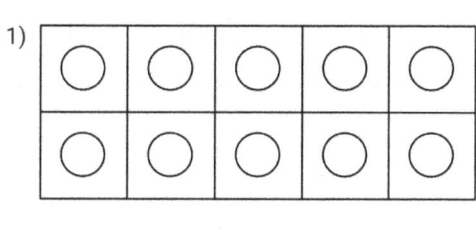

1)   2)

7   5

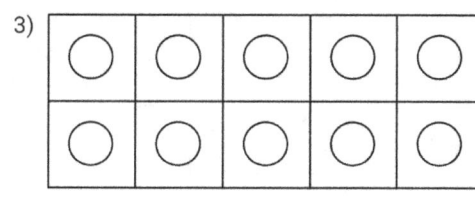 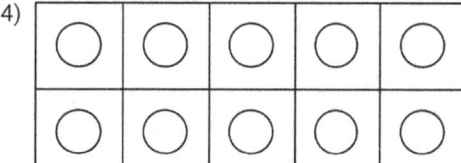

2   10

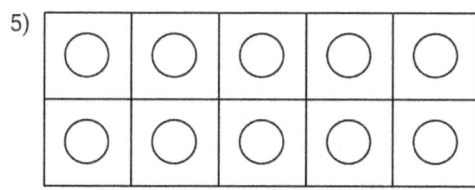 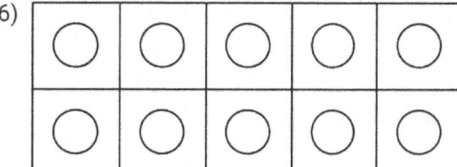

4   8

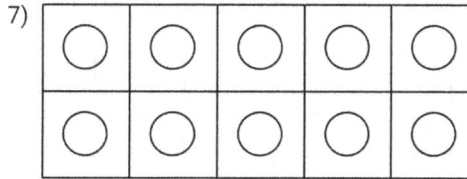 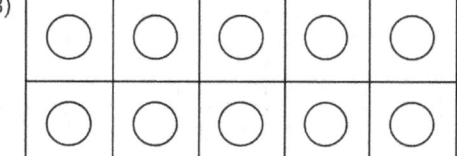

3   1

Counting

Color the counters to match the number shown.

1) 6

2) 10

3) 8

4) 5

5) 4

6) 1

7) 2

8) 9

Counting

Color the counters to match the number shown.

1)

2

2)

10

3)

5

4)

9

5)

3

6)

10

7)

1

8)

4

Missing Numbers

Fill the missing numbers and color the picture.

Missing Numbers

Fill the missing numbers and color the picture.

Missing Numbers

Fill the missing numbers and color the picture.

Missing Numbers

Fill the missing numbers and color the picture.

Missing Numbers

Fill the missing numbers and color the picture.

Missing Numbers

Fill the missing numbers and color the picture.

www.ingramcontent.com/pod-product-compliance
Lightning Source LLC
Chambersburg PA
CBHW060426010526
44118CB00017B/2374